THE 12 PRINCIPLES OF SUSTAINABILITY

MILLARD ARTERBERRY

EDENFINITY
edenfinity.org

Book design by Nuno Moreira, NMDESIGN.ORG
ISBN: 978-0-578-95426-4

THE 12 PRINCIPLES OF SUSTAINABILITY

AN ESSAY

ON OUR RELATIONSHIP

WITH EARTH

MILLARD ARTERBERRY

Contents

Acknowledgments

While many amazing ideas from many amazing people has shaped this essay, the following people have had the most profound influence on this essay, but it is these people and their work have had these 12 principles:

Christopher Alexander's course and book *The Nature of Order* was by far the most life changing class I ever took. While the ostensible goal of his teaching was to illuminate the process of designing order and beauty, his ideas reshaped the way I looked at life. This book could not possibly exist without his concepts.

Guy Murchie's many works, most notably *The Seven Mysteries Of Life*, is not only part of the foundation of this work, it is essential reading for any truth seeker. Mr. Murchie writes with simplicity and humility, breaking down deep esoteric concepts into very readable language. An independent thinker of the highest quality.

Jack Kornfield's *Your Buddha Nature* quite simply changed my life. I grew up in the catholic religion, going to catholic school and attending church every Sunday. I drifted away from organized religion in my 20's but *Your Buddha Nature* helped me rediscover virtue and compassion., the soul of this book.

Preface

The seed of this book was planted in the early 2000's when I noticed many people and companies exploiting the words "sustainable" and "green" to sell something. I realized there was no clear definition of these words in the environmentally friendly context. A quest to define sustainability for myself grew into The 12 Principles Of Sustainability.

This essay is not based on any religious or political dogma; it is based on a lifetime of reading and research—not just about sustainability, but history, philosophy, and art. I included many of my personal experiences in this essay, many very difficult. I know many people who were given far fewer gifts than I and have faced many more challenges. My experiences with adversity and personal loss, however, were intrinsic to the formation of these principles. They tempered and strengthened them in a way only these kinds of experiences can.

Ultimately, I wrote this essay for myself in the honest pursuit of truth. There has been tremendous healing in the process of distilling these ideas from my skills and experience, and knowing that it may contribute to healing this world.

This book is dedicated to

Sylvia Arterberry & Millard Nathan Arterberry Sr.

The Path to the Principles

1

This book was written for people like myself, who care deeply about the compromised state of our environment and would like to contribute to its healing but do not know where to start.

This book is not based on decades of hard work in the trenches of environmental justice; it emerged from my need to define sustainability for myself and ground the trajectory of my action in bedrock principles.

I wish I could claim a methodical, scientific origin for the principles I am proposing here, but I can't. There was nothing planned about developing the principles of sustainability. They were born almost by accident and grew in a lot of sunshine and rain.

2

Growing up, I was blessed to be a part of a church community that really looked out for its members. We were a Catholic family. We went to church every Sunday and attended Catholic school. I remember the holidays and the yearly carnival, and so many good people who would give you the clothes off their back if you needed it. What I treasured most, though, was the feeling of belonging to a tight-knit community. Even though I am no longer Catholic, the morals and sense of community in our parish still have a profound effect on my worldview.

I also had the good fortune to be a part of an amazing extended family. My father was born in a small, historically black town in Oklahoma, and he had 14 children in his family. As a result, I have over forty first cousins, who travel back to Oklahoma every Memorial day to celebrate family. Being a part of the Arterberry clan has been a tremendous blessing.

In my senior year of high school, I unilaterally decided to part ways with the traditional educational system, choosing instead to attend the University of Downtown Tijuana, where I majored in partying like it was my job. After a couple of years of this, with no diploma and no job, I went to the family farm in Oklahoma for six months. It was very strange for a San Diego boy, living in a tiny town of about sixty people, but I guess it got something to click inside me. I learned a lot of things there, maybe most importantly, that I needed to figure out a way to make money with my mind. When I learned that my grandfather had built most of the homes in this little town, I was inspired to study architecture.

After kissing the ground in relief when I got back to San Diego, I got my GED and enrolled in community college. Luckily, the college I attended had an excellent matriculation program with the UC system, so after a couple of years, I could transfer to UC Berkeley, where I graduated with honors with a degree in architecture in 1995.

3

I didn't care much about sustainability in school or at the beginning of my career. After a few years in the business, I made a decent living and married to a wonderful girl. I didn't think very far beyond my own little corner of the world until I really started analyzing what I was doing for a living.

A lot of our clients were developers who built and sold tract homes. They would buy large pieces of land, subdivide them into a few hundred lots, then scrap everything off the land and plunk down the same three or four designs over and over again. It's hard to explain the feeling of revulsion I had when I understood what I was a part of. I was party to spawning acres and acres of hollow human containers, with no thought of creating a real community or doing anything unique, challenging, or world-changing. The designs we used were decades-old, just spruced up a little, and spat out for a quick profit. Even though I knew nothing about "green" or "sustainable," I knew there had to be a more meaningful way to build homes.

My employment didn't improve much, but I started researching green homes and sustainable design on my own. It was such a revelation!

I came to understand that there have been extraordinary minds designing great, sustainable projects for decades. For whatever reason, their work received very little public attention compared to higher-profile projects that focused on superficial aesthetics and profit.

I loved this research. After about a year, I found the United States Green Building Council online and their LEED professional accreditation program. A few weeks after, I tested for and received my LEED accreditation, and was excited to get started on real, sustainable projects.

Even though I had moved on from tract homes in a new job, there was little interest in sustainability in the firm in which I worked at the time. My initial enthusiasm waned as I faced the fact that, being just an employee, I had little say in what projects I worked on, or whether they would include sustainable elements. On top of that, I had a family to feed.

After a year of increasingly professional frustration, I decided to enter a sustainable home design competition, sponsored by the city of Henderson, Nevada. Keep in mind that I had been given almost no opportunity to design after seven or eight years in the business, even though I had studied under one of the best design minds in the world. All I had was several years of learning the nuts and bolts of the business. Somehow, I channeled some wax-on wax-off magic and won the competition. I then resolved to start my own firm to ensure I had control over the projects on which I worked. Up to that point, my career had been easy—I almost always had enough work, I had money in the bank, and I felt like I was ready for the next challenge. What could go wrong?

Well, as it turns out, quite a bit.

4

It was around 2006 that my Dark Night of the Soul began. It sounds like a terrible thing to happen to someone, but it's actually much worse than it sounds. It's an endless black abyss with no escape. None. No matter what you do. All you do is survive and pray. My version of this was a series of three events in succession that completely upended my world.

The first event was the near-collapse of my marriage. I married a beautiful woman, who was the perfect girl for me, and after a seven-year courtship and two years of marriage, we had a wonderful daughter. After being in an incredible relationship for nine years, I had not thought that it would ever be different or end—but four years later, we were on the brink of breaking up. It was only through very, very difficult and painful work that we were able to salvage our marriage.

Perhaps a month after my marriage had stabilized to the point where I felt it might survive, my little sister died. It wasn't just a call in the night, either. The road to my sister's death was a painful trek of several months.

My sister was seven years younger than me—just 32. When she had come home from the hospital as a newborn, I had sat on the bed next to her, just staring. My sister was a genuinely good-hearted, talented person who worked as a dialysis nurse and had a family with three children. She was so good at her job and helped so many people. She left a devastated family.

5

It was a few weeks after my sister's service that I resolved to start my own firm. I realized that tomorrow is promised to no one, and I might as well accomplish whatever it is I plan on accomplishing in this lifetime.

Unfortunately, I made this decision in late 2007, which happened to be the absolute worst time to start a home design business. In early 2008, the stock and housing market crashed, and opportunities for projects evaporated. I had taken a lot of time off to deal with my marriage and my sister's passing, so my finances were already stretched. After six months of no work, I was out of money and facing a pile of bills that I had no idea how to pay.

Life became a daily grind of waking up, spending four hours looking for a job, and then spending the next four hours keeping my CAD skills sharp. Work did come sporadically, just enough to get by, but not enough to avoid two downsizes. I was somebody with a valuable skill set who was ready and able to work, but could not find any. To me, that seemed very indicative of a fundamental flaw in the system in which I was participating. Financial pressure can be crushing, but economic pressure compounded by a family depending on you is crushing times a million.

My dark night lasted for five years. There were happy moments, but pressure and struggle were always there. Real hope proved to be elusive.

Despite the struggle, I continued to research sustainability. My research took a turn when I sought funding to build my award-winning design as a spec home for profit. By that point, my credit was shot, so there was no way anyone would loan me money. But, in a conversation with a loan broker, he asked me a question that pivoted my entire thinking on sustainability. When he saw my design and how much money I asked for, he asked me, "Why are you just building one house?".

After he looked at my financials, he let me know that, unless I walked out his door and tripped over a $2,000,000 bill, I was probably not going to get funding. His question persisted in my mind, though, and I did my due diligence to research any advantages to building multiple homes as opposed to just one. The economy had kicked me around so much that I hadn't dared to think big in years.

I jumped into this new line of sustainable inquiry and realized quickly that, due to several factors, communities had far greater sustainable potential than individual homes. I came to believe that small neighborhood-sized communities would be pivotal in transforming our population into a genuinely sustainable world community.

Like my research with green techniques for individual home building, I found so many great solutions to virtually every problem our species faces. I found multiple creative solutions for food and energy production, water sourcing, responsible consumer goods sourcing, composting, and zero-waste strategies—it was so heartening to see that all these great ideas were out there.

I decided to write a book on the importance of small-scale sustainable community building. I had actually typed about four chapters before I hit a huge wall. I couldn't figure out my way forward for a day or two until it dawned on me—I couldn't write this book. As much as I had learned in my studies, I had not built a sustainable community, nor had I ever lived in one. Anything I wrote would be a farce.

I was about to set aside the manuscript for good, when I reread my first chapter. In it, I did something I had longed to do for years—define sustainability for myself. I noticed a lot of "green" and "sustainable" products and services being marketed all the time, but it was clear there was no precise definition for these terms—just a vague sense that they were "good for the environment."

I knew early on that I needed to anchor this writing in principle. This meant that the definition of sustainability could flow very naturally into principles people could use to determine whether or not something is genuinely sustainable. There was not much volume there, but it was pithy and captured so much of what I had learned through hard experience.

6

My aborted book venture happened when I was still dealing with some of my greatest challenges. In 2011, I found work in Las Vegas and left my family in San Diego to rent a room in the Nevada desert. After about three months, the projects ran out, and I had to return home with just a few thousand dollars in my pocket. I began work on a small home improvement project that lasted about a month. When I finished the project, I had no money left—at all. I'll never forget that day.

I finished in the afternoon. I cleaned up, then sat on the couch and just paused. I realized I was 45, had no job and no money, and the economy was still iffy at best. Yet, for some reason, I felt a deep calm come over me. I realized the constant tension and inner struggle I had experienced for five years was gone. I didn't consciously do anything to make it go away; it just wasn't there anymore.

I went outside to take a walk in the park across the street from my place. I decided to talk to the Universe—no begging, no whining; I realized I didn't want or need to anymore. I simply said I still have skills, and I would like to use those skills to contribute something meaningful. I couldn't do it without help, so I asked for some assistance.

Moments after I asked this, I got a call from my wife's friend. She wanted me to build her a website and would give me a down payment for it. The down payment would be helpful, in that I had no working computer.

Even though websites were not my main gig, it was something I had done occasionally to earn money between architectural jobs. I got the money, bought a computer, and made the website. That led me to few more web projects, including a website for an aborted UFO movie project centered on a place called Giant Rock in the middle of the Mojave Desert; it was just enough money to get me by for a few months until I realized I needed to get back into architecture.

I was out of practice and still psychologically scarred, but I resolved to find an architectural job. Even after I found two jobs that didn't work out, I persevered, and in September of 2013, I responded to an ad for an architectural position in Sausalito, just across the Golden Gate Bridge from San Francisco. I came to Sausalito with nothing more than the first month's rent for a small room to my name. I had to leave my family behind again.

The Universe smiled on me in Sausalito. After a year, I could move my family here, and we were very fortunate to find a wonderful place to live with a great view. In 2017, I could start my own firm, and I eventually hired a few employees.

I've spent my seven years in Sausalito becoming human again, slowly letting go of all the trauma I experienced. Even though I have my own firm, my need to play financial catchup caused me to sometimes compromise my belief in the necessity of sustainable design, though not always.

7

And so I find myself in the momentous year of 2020. A small window of opportunity to bring the ideas that grew in my darkest hours into the light has presented itself, and I choose to jump through it. It is with deep gratitude that I now share these principles with you. They were written with the deeply held belief that, despite our collective Dark Night of the Soul, the dawn is coming.

Principle #1

"Sustainable" is that which contributes to the establishment and continuance of a symbiotic, regenerative, and indefinitely sustainable relationship between our species and our planet.

"Green" and "sustainable" are commonly used interchangeably as catchall adjectives that describe a relatively broad range of ideas, practices, products, and services. While "green" for our purposes remains somewhat nebulous, "sustainable" has a far more specific meaning in relation to how we live on this planet.

Sustainability is very easy to understand—it is rooted in our survival instinct, and it is our ability as a species to survive and thrive indefinitely on this planet.

Sustainability is NOT about saving this planet. What a complete fantasy. This planet can manage just fine without us saving her. If I saw humanity coming around the corner looking like it wanted to save me, I would turn around and run top speed the other way.

Sustainability is about saving ourselves from ourselves. We disobeyed the cardinal rule of nature, which is not to poop in your own nest. With 7.8 billion of us pooping away, we have made a terrible, terrible mess.

As such, sustainability is a species-wide challenge to modify our behavior so that, for all cities and regions on our planet, the sum of their activities maintain or enhance a given region's ecological balance.

A system like this does not deplete the resources of a given region over time; it carefully calibrates human activity with resource availability and maintenance of native flora and fauna so that human activities can sustain themselves indefinitely over time.

Principle #2

Our World is a Living Being Inhabiting a Universe of Living Energy

Many of us can intuit this reality now, far more than in past decades. This is in large part thanks to our modern physicists, whose work has slowly and steadily trickled into our common consciousness. So many ideas most of us assumed to be true—materialism, the dumb and dead vacuum of space, an object-based reality—have long-since been eclipsed by far more interesting discoveries in astrophysics and quantum mechanics. Here are some highlights:

- The underlying substrate of the Universe is anything but a vacuum. It is a living, conscious energy field whereby the point of consciousness each one of us experiences is the streaming, holographic, multi-sensory sensations we call life.

- This Life Energy Field is at once a container for life and life itself. The objects, plants, animals, and people that we see only exist for us as energetic potential. That is, until our act of observation changes them into vibrating concentrations of energy that our minds interpret as hidden objects. The deeper reality, however, is that we are observing one field, one matrix, and one big bowl of energy soup, of which we are an intrinsic part.

- We vibrate concentrations of energy within and a part of this field. If we liken ourselves to a theater, we are both the projector and the audience.

- Our reaction to what we experience in this field—for instance, our emotional state—is directly related to our vibratory state.

- We project holographic thoughtforms, whose content is dependent on our vibratory level, and both the "screen" and your vibratory level react and adjust to each other. This is life. Quantum physics has shown that what we experience as a continuum is actually a strobing series of thoughtforms morphing slightly every moment.

- Perhaps the most essential characteristic of the Universe for our purposes is flow. The motion of the Universe is how

> we experience time and events. As a result of Universal Flow, everything in the Universe is in a constant state of flux—either growing or decaying. How sustainable a given energy concentration or system is will be determined, not just by static structural characteristics, but by how energy flows through it.

This is the reality into which you were born. You live in a beautiful place, and you have the power to sculpt it to your taste. One caveat, though: with power comes responsibility.

Principle #3

The Primary Characteristics of Sustainability Are Environmental Harmony, Environmental Efficiency, and Environmental Quality

From the root drive of survival and the need to develop a positive relationship with our environment, we can extrapolate three characteristics of true sustainability:

- Environmental Harmony
- Environmental Efficiency
- Environmental Quality

These aspects are fundamental qualities of Vital Living Systems that interweave and overlap with each other. Let's take a deep dive into each one.

Environmental Harmony

Environmental Harmony may be best described as developing a symbiotic relationship with all our bioregions and the planet as a whole. Every bioregion on the planet is a unique system whose environment is formed by a delicate interplay of landform, climate, animals, and plants. In an ideal symbiotic relationship, plants and animals are adapted to the given landscape and climate and form an interdependent food chain, which creates a sustainable energetic balance over time.

In almost every instance, the presence of modern cities has severely disrupted the host bioregion. Resource depletion, pollution, and climate change are just some of the adverse effects that cities have on our planet's biomes. In most cases, the basic resource utilization systems we have developed are not in harmony with nature and thus are not sustainable over time.

The inevitable result is obvious: if we continue to relate to our environment in our current manner, our resources will eventually deplete, and the planet will be polluted beyond the point of being able to sustain our civilization at its current size and development level.

Environmental Harmony entails a commitment to scientifically studying the natural systems of each watershed and bioregion, determining a comfortable maximum human population a given bioregion can support, and then redesigning our resource systems to complement those of nature.

Environmental Efficiency

Nature rewards efficiency.

When our resource utilization is in harmony with natural processes, we rely on the earth to provide us with abundance. The price of this abundance is the responsibility of using these resources as efficiently as possible.

This means that we must extract only the amount of a given resource so as not to cause the resource to deplete over time. This applies particularly to organic sources. Mineral sources that are mined will inevitably deplete in any given region. As such, there must be a comprehensive plan in place to reuse and recycle the products produced by these materials to the greatest extent possible.

It is also our responsibility to extract, process, and use our energy, water, and food with maximum efficiency. An abundant lifestyle is not in conflict with an efficient system, but a wasteful one is.

Environmental Quality

Harmonious and efficient systems may be sustainable, but Environmental Quality is what makes it truly worth sustaining. If the environments that we live in are not pleasing to the eye, and if they do not support happy healthy lives, what is the point of being harmonious and efficient?

Any sustainable strategy must be one that puts the quality of life ahead of everything else. All too often, the myth is repeated that being eco-friendly is about sacrificing convenience and money to "save the planet." Unfortunately, ideas like this are passed along by many well-meaning environmentalists who often focus only on efficiency, mainly because it is the easiest sell in a materialistic society organized around a fight for artificially limited resources.

It may sound foreign and unrealistic to most who struggle and work to survive, but real-life quality for everyone on this planet is attainable. The technological and natural resources are here; we just have to implement them intelligently and equitably.

Principle #4

A Sustainable Community Is a Vital Living System

When a community is in harmony with its environment, when it uses its resources efficiently, and when its members enjoy abundant happy lives, this community can be said to be a Vital Living System.

While we all exist within the same energy field, which is conscious and alive everywhere, then varying degrees of vitality exist at different locations. The phenomenon of vitality degrees is a more profound idea than merely organic life versus inanimate objects. Everything exhibits some level of vitality, including inorganic objects, and this is reflected in the relative beauty and order of a given object or entity. The degree of vitality shares a strong congruence with the degree of sustainability.

Contrast can help us understand the concept. Think of a healthy rainforest, pristine desert, or even a beautiful, well-planted neighborhood. When we experience these spaces, we sense the vitality and are drawn to it, just as places like the enormous dump that has accumulated in the middle of the Pacific Ocean repel us. While it is not always easy to determine the specific characteristics that differentiate living and diseased systems, we all instinctively recognize both.

Principle #5

Sustainable Forms Derive from Sustainable, Structure-preserving Processes.

While it is vital to understand sustainability characteristics, to evolve our communities, we must understand the processes that create sustainability. These processes are as varied as life, but they all may be described as "structure-preserving transformations," as defined by Christopher Alexander in his magnum opus book *The Nature Of Order.*

Our first instinct in confronting challenges is often to focus on fixing what is not working, or even blowing everything up and starting from scratch. The quickest and surest path to sustainability, however, is to assess our systems to determine what works and then employing our resources to these elements to enhance them. Even the most corrupt, rotting system has some parts that work.

When the desired incremental, positive change has been achieved, we simply repeat the process—assess what works, then deploy assets to enhance them. Sustainable change is structure-preserving, not disruptive. It is evolution, not revolution.

Principle #6

The Rights of Life, Sustenance, Vitality, and Freedom of Expression are Inherent to All Humans. With These Rights Comes the Responsibility of Contribution to the Nurturing of These Rights for All.

The first part of this principle has been stated similarly many times, and I will simply assume these truths to be self-evident.

The same thing can be said about the second part, which is just a natural consequence of the Golden Rule—do unto others as you would have them do unto you. We have all heard this many times, and somehow, we have also all managed to forget it many times in our lives. This principle is indispensable to sustainability.

Principle #7

No Community can Achieve True Sustainability at the Expense of Another Community.

In our current consumer paradigm, artificially induced scarcity to work drives us, and we buy and consume endlessly just to survive. For most people on this planet, time given to producing life quality is a luxury that cannot be afforded while basic survival is on the line. This reality is increasingly apparent—not just in developing countries but also in the more developed "first world" countries. The bell is beginning to toll for the eroded middle-class of our prosperous nations, and we are starting to have a tiny taste of the pressure and struggle that billions face every day in places like Monrovia, Lagos, Colombo, and Sao Paolo.

Our consumerist culture is dependent on market first world countries that live in relative comfort from supplier third world countries providing raw materials and goods. The system is propped up by rigged elections, assassinations, brutal repression of organized labor, and the might of the most powerful military the world has ever seen spread over hundreds of bases worldwide.

When one group step on the neck of another, an imbalance is created, and the pressure to rebalance grows until there is either system correction or system failure. Imbalances such as this are inherently unsustainable. True environmental quality in one part of the system cannot come at the expense of another part of the system. As long as we have governments and corporate systems that leave vast chunks of the population stuck in generational poverty and squalor, we do not have sustainability.

Principle #8

Sustainable Communities Dynamically Balance the Interests of the Commons with the Interests of the Individual.

Most of us have experienced one or more economic crashes in our lifetime. Over the last four decades, the quality of life for most Americans has degraded significantly. Many point to this as an inevitable consequence of the death of rapacious capitalism. Proponents of social programs see our best chance of emerging whole from the growing crisis as replacing "capitalism" with "socialism," while proponents of capitalism continue to defend the laissez-faire system.

Both arguments suffer under the faulty belief that capitalism and socialism are two wholly different systems. In fact, they are not stand-alone economic systems, but rather dynamics within every human community directly from two characteristics inherent within all humans: self-interest and cooperation. Capitalism is self-interest in action, just as socialism is the direct manifestation of the common good drive.

Every human community has elements of both these characteristics. Both are absolutely necessary for a sustainable community, and neither will ever go away as long as people are people. Both can be extremely destructive in excess, and a healthy, sustainable society must continually balance these forces through assessment and adjustment.

Principle #9

There Is No Such Thing As Waste

There is no waste in a sustainable paradigm. Period. The practice of burying, burning, or dumping our by-products into the ocean is no longer a viable solution, if they ever were.

Every by-product stream we currently bury, burn, or dump into the ocean must be integrated back into our life, sustaining systems through reuse, recycling, and composting.

Principle #10

Sustainability Over Time is Dependent on Efficient and Sustainable Resource Flow

Principles such as harmony, efficiency, and life quality are high-minded goals, but to understand sustainability in practice, we have to track how our communities obtain, use, and dispose of resources. A Resource Flow Chart showing all resource inputs and outputs to a given community system is a means of graphically modeling these functions, and is extremely useful in seeing how sustainable principles can be applied over time.

Principle #11

Sustainable Communities Proceed From Dependence to Independence, and, Ultimately, to Interdependence

Dependence is a healthy condition during the establishment period of any community. We were all dependent on parents or guardians in our infancy and childhood—not just for food and a home, but also for our worldview. This unidirectional flow of energy is necessary for protection and growth, but at some point, these must give way to independence or sink into co-dependence.

An independent community is one that is self-reliant and autonomous. It can grow its own food, build its own houses, and generate its own energy. Like dependence, independence is a healthy condition in its proper time, but can eventually lead to isolation if the next stage of development is not achieved.

Interdependence is the ideal end-state for a community. Interdependent components within any system are ultimately self-reliant but do create limited dependencies with other communities for mutual benefit, taking advantage of the synergies available by combining with other communities to form larger organizations.

Every stage of development has pitfalls, including interdependence, but this last stage is essential for any community to achieve sustainability.

Principle #12

Compassion and Service are the Only Lasting Foundations of Community

Many people throughout history have stated the fundamental importance of compassion to our human community. To wit:

"Love and compassion are necessities, not luxuries. Without them, humanity cannot survive."

Dalia Lama XIV

"A human being is a part of the whole called by us universe, a part limited in time and space. He experiences himself, his thoughts and feeling as something separated from the rest, a kind of optical delusion of his consciousness. This delusion is a kind of prison for us, restricting us to our personal desires and to affection for a few persons nearest to us. Our task must be to free ourselves from this prison by widening our circle of compassion to embrace all living creatures and the whole of nature in its beauty."

Albert Einstein

"True compassion is more than flinging a coin to a beggar; it comes to see that an edifice which produces beggars needs restructuring."

Dr. Martin Luther King, Jr.

"Without justice and love, peace will always be a great illusion."

Dom Helder Camara

"If a free society cannot help the many who are poor, it cannot save the few who are rich."

John Fitzgerald Kennedy

"A mature person is one who does not think only in absolutes, who is able to be objective even when deeply stirred emotionally, who has learned that there is both good and bad in all people and in all things, and who walks humbly and deals charitably with the circumstances of life, knowing that in this world no one is all-knowing and therefore all of us need both love and charity."

Eleanor Roosevelt

The Universal Field in which we find ourselves is recursive—what we project into it is what will be ultimately reflected back to us. If our goal is inner and outer equanimity, the ideal emotion to project out into the Universe is compassion.

Compassion is simply unconditional love. It is based on a deep knowledge of the oneness of all things and the nature of that which binds us. The heart of compassion looks in the face of your friends and enemies alike and sees yourself reflected back. The eyes of compassion see from the heart and do not judge but recognize the humanness of everyone.

Nothing is sustainable without compassion; yet how many constitutions mention it? Our civilization is centered in our heads and has little use for compassion. Countries continue to struggle, war and pass into history without ever realizing that compassion is the only foundation that lasts.

Vision

1

As I write these lines I can look out from my balcony in Sausalito and see thick smoke covering all of San Francisco Bay. A few days prior I drove from Washington to California during the night, with almost the entire way covered in smoke. In southern Oregon I was actually able to see the flames of a fire front stretching for miles just a few hundred feet from the freeway; I learned later that stretch of freeway closed minutes after I passed the border into California. When I reached the Bay Area everything was covered with a seemingly endless pall of smoke that made the entire sky a dark apocalyptic orange. It stretched from Sacramento 60+ miles all the way to the bay. I had never seen anything like it.

2020 has been a year of a health crisis, a crippling shutdown of our economy, the largest protests in U.S. history in answer to racially based police violence, a terrible hurricane, and the destructive fires I witnessed first-hand along the west coast.

We are seeing the death throes of our old world. The institutions that we built to safeguard our life, liberty and property no longer serve us, and they will all either adapt or die. If we choose to participate in the birth of the new world our charge is to create and hold a vision of that beautiful new world and contribute whatever energy we can to its manifestation, all as the aging edifices slowly crumble around us, and the masks melt away from the Cowards That Be. *A* world is ending, but *The* World is not. If we maintain our vision of a sustainable world in the face of fear and chaos, we will see the other side of the darkness.

2

Humanity right now has the capacity to create a worldwide, sustainable, democratic infrastructure, that feeds, houses and provides a strong base quality of life for everybody on the planet. If built in alignment with underlying natural laws, this infrastructure will also address the severe degradation and resulting climate change this biome has experienced at our hands. We have all the available manpower, knowledge and technological capacity necessary to accomplish this.

I have no idea whether the Garden of Eden was in our past. I do however believe it is our destiny if we so choose.

The major impediment to the implementation of a more just, sustainable civilization has always been our greed and selfishness. This manifests in our inequitable resource distribution systems that rely on artificial scarcity to spike short term profits for an increasingly small percentage of the population. The system is kept in place by a corporate stranglehold on resource systems and the government institutions designed to police big business.

This stranglehold will only be broken by a critical mass of citizens actively, tangibly, physically participating in the creation of our new world. This not just a call to meditate and bliss out every day. We all have an obligation to contribute to the construction of the new platform for our civilization. There is no one person or organization who has all the answers, but collectively we all have answers.

My chosen path of contribution will be researching, building and advocating for Local Resource Independence. Our local neighborhood and village sized communities have the power to grow their own food, produce their own energy and provide their own capital.

The best way to slay the beast confronting us is to starve it. Disengaging from the unhealthy dependent relationship we share with big business and big government will allow all parties to redefine themselves in a more sustainable manner. True sustainability will require solutions at all scales of community, but tackling the challenge at the village and neighborhood level can be a tremendous catalyst for the larger and smaller scales.

We are an adolescent civilization stumbling through a nightmare of our own making. Yet our highest path is still available to us: to choose to become responsible stewards of the Garden.

3

In 2010 I was still reeling from personal and financial loss from the 2008 crash. I had been a spiritual seeker for most of my 20s and 30s, and tried many paths to regain my center amid terrible uncertainty and depression. I tried everything I knew to overcome my situation. The struggle did keep me and my family alive and off the street, but just barely. Every month seemed a little more difficult, and normalcy drifted further and further from reach.

It was in this state that a friend gave me a set of audio tapes of lectures by Jack Kornfield entitled "Your Buddha Nature: Teachings On The Ten Perfections". It was several hours long, and I listened to those tapes over and over for many months. They took my mind away from the constant struggle to stay afloat and shifted it to becoming a better person.

It was these lessons derived from the Buddha that inspired me to design a meditation to seed my life with compassion. I practiced that meditation daily for a year, flooding myself with compassionate energy. The result of this was something that must be experienced to be appreciated.

In my various spiritual practices I had many mysterious experiences, but I never felt the ground shift beneath my feet until I consciously brought compassion into my being. I still have problems, life is still life, but I was fundamentally better off for the change.

This practice provided the foundation for everything I have done since (well, maybe not *everything*). I have a long, long way to go before I can truly say I fully live a life of compassionate service, but I know it is the right path.

I'm bringing up compassion one last time because it is that important to sustainability. Sustainability is not about solar panels or climate change, or revolting against the 1%. At its deepest level it is enough of us making a personal life commitment of service to a cause greater than self.

About The Author

Millard Arterberry is a native of San Diego, CA. Graduating from the University of California at Berkeley in 1995 with a degree in architecture, Millard has spent a 25-year career working in several architectural firms. He is an award-winning LEED accredited professional.

In 2017, he opened his own home design firm.

He currently lives in Sausalito, CA, with his wife of twenty years and his daughter.

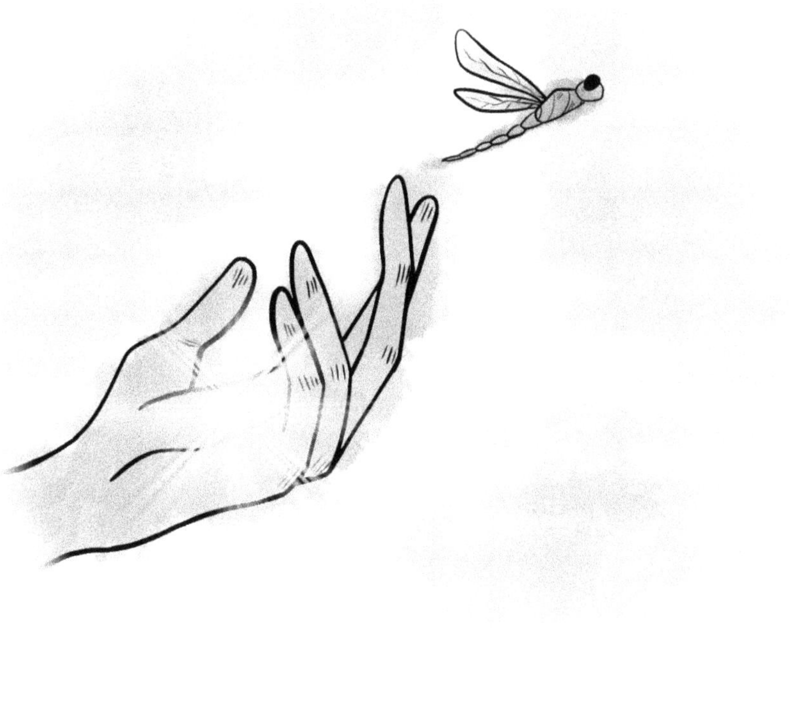

Lightning Source UK Ltd.
Milton Keynes UK
UKHW022337250223
417423UK00024B/61

9 780578 954264